PREVIOUSLY UNSEEN

Paul L Quant

Copyright © 2013 Lulu Author. All rights reserved.

ISBN 978 –1–291–47224-0

Dedication

To Benjamin, Abigail and Laurence

Author's Note

I have come to realise that 'people-watching' can be a rewarding and life-affirming experience. These poems, written loosely in sonnet form, came from fleeting glances at people I did not know. My understanding of them was speculative; but isn't that the way we initially relate to people?

Paul L Quant

March 2013

Previously Unseen

Anybody There?

She has long hair. I cannot see her face
But realise she's taken out her phone
Like millions of the present human race
Who seem to be much of the time alone.
Her fingers play around the tiny keys
An urgency her skipping mind maintains
To quickly find one listener to please
Pick up the message that her hand contains.
But there is something that she cannot place,
However swift her telephoning style;
She cannot share the look upon his face,
The charm, surprise, the measure of his smile,
Until she opens up the kitchen door
And holds his outstretched hand in hers once more.

Was He Spanish?

Both in a hurry, we shot down the path,
Shops shut and more important things to do
So when I looked at him a camera's glance
Was all I had to go on, get into
His Spanish ways, his Spanish soul, his pride,
Things given him by years under the sun.
But now in England had another side
Wiped out the special times when he was young?
I couldn't ask him; that would be unfair,
For never had I seen him, couldn't tell
What baked-hard earth and olives growing there
Affected him for worse or very well.
I feel a chance had gone to know the truth
About the lad, the handsome Spanish youth.

Previously Unseen

At the Railway Station

No hiss of steaming engine, slamming doors,
No signals move, no level crossing men,
No saddle-engines now, no four-two-fours:
Those memories will not come back again.
Why does he work here still, without the points
Moved smoothly by a man in true command?
Why face the diesel engines' creaking joints
Once coal-fired juggernauts had fled the land?
He seemed to be some ancient dinosaur
In wide-brimmed cap, tweed coat and cycle-clips,
So out-of-touch with managements at war
On railways and the way they come to grips
With novelty that modern times arrange –
He still works there? That seems so very strange.

Up and Down the Street

How do you judge bones of integrity?
Fold back the box lid, contents there assess?
I tell you, if that task were up to me,
I'd settle for a motley, curious mess.
He stared and spied on all the people who
Ignored him, didn't even recognise
That man whose secret look was fixed by glue
And stamped unpleasant in his devious eyes.
Deep subterfuge like that he practised till
Nobody knew that danger was his game.
The sun is set behind each local hill
With its profound and decade-polished grain.
You, even though you think you'll crack his code,
Be wary, for I am the open road.

Previously Unseen

Trolley Collector

His employment seemed unusual, oddly placed,
Collecting trolleys, large and small from where
The supermarket customers had graced
The car park zone and left them empty, bare.
Not intellectually-challenged, he could be
A charming conversationalist and
A helpful man who everyone could see
Was keen to demonstrate the product's brand.
For all the while and up and down outside
The smart shop he'd be busy, everywhere
Intending to express the corporate pride
Expected of him and with consummate care
He'd do more than was asked: his feet had wings.
He loved the space that stacking trolleys brings.

Builder's Mate

He's usually calmly, strongly helping out
The builder who pays wages for his toil;
He seldom speaks when I go thereabouts
To seek his boss, their harmony to spoil.
Wrapped up through winter's cold and rainy spells
The two of them transform the aged house,
Get rid of rubbish with its musty smells
And laugh a little sometimes, maybe grouse
About the job, the wife, the cost of stuff.
But when I join them, down the curtain comes;
Their solitude for them has time enough
That others coming seem like warring drums.
One smiles in affability, although
The lesser man's eyes challenge, 'Please just go!'

Previously Unseen

Chip Van Man

A well-washed, well-brushed, well-dressed man,
A model of his tribe, white overall,
A once-a-week-come-hither selling plan
With fish and chips his trade. We hear his call
Sound out whenever he pulls to the kerb
Across the road. The steaming chimney tries
To tantalize the customers he serves -
Fish smells, the cod, the haddock, peas and pies.
He stands alone, hands folded. Minutes pass
Until it's clear he's wanted here no more.
He shuts the hatch, sits down, looks in the glass;
The engine starts, his foot upon the floor.
Around the corner, stop, begin again;
A thankless job when there is pouring rain.

The Italian

A party, on his own and at the side,
An introduction; we were set to speak.
A handsome face, head lifted high to pride;
His thrown-off home he sees now not so bleak.
A family man, eyes shining, telling of
The summers when the fields of olives sang
Of shimmering light, the sun hung high above
The steep hills with white rock an overhang,
His house outside the small town. Could he feel
Life overseas without a micro-sense
Of hard regret? I saw no blind appeal,
No heart of distant banter, no intense
And social harvest. No border was crossed;
Too many trails of contact stung by frost.

Previously Unseen

Such Long and Curly Hair

Such long and curly hair on one so sharp,
The over-looking man with book in hand.
Words roll beneath his stroking fingers' harp
Like gentle hills in summer's hazy land.
I do not know his background, what had fired
To bring his thinking through the written word,
With which his spirit seemed to be inspired
In book and book and line on line inferred.
Perhaps he dreamed or dreaded leaving here
Bereft of understanding what was real
In everything he hoped might show up clear:
The essence of what human beings feel.
No, maybe selling books was what he did
To pass the time and earn an honest quid.

Street Musician

An amplifier and a smart guitar
Were weapons to this little cloth-capped man
Who crouched upon a case as if at war.
No wonder I became a ready fan,
For chords and riffs and melodies galore
He played with easy fingers, easy style.
The passing shoppers heard him long before
They saw him playing in the shopping mall
But something of his outer confidence
Confused me when I stood nearby and watched
Him totally ignore each twenty pence
Thrown in his hat but, oh so gently, touched
The instrument that sang aloud his mood,
As if it offered him his daily food.

Previously Unseen

Dog walking man

The timing doesn't change. He goes outside
All weathers, the same route, just like a bus,
Led by his fine companion, with the tide
Going out, then in, like all of us
For even though we think we dive and swim
Upon the day's dimensions all about
We rarely feel the winds tickle our skin;
Complexities of life don't find us out.
So don't deride the dog man as he strolls
On even footpaths. All around the town
The houses, shops, the old electric poles
Do lift him up, not knock his spirits down.
I watch him come and go and slightly smile
Then turn back to my book, as is my style.

Fen Dweller

He wasn't from those parts and didn't stick
His flag onto our ways, our close contract;
Drove a strange car that stuttered, sounded sick
And worked away from home where he could act
More as himself, where others, too, felt safe
With strangeness, difference and solitude,
Where sympathetic tones were taken for
Essential kindness, not like foreign food
A salesman brings to sell at your front door.
His son spent time with mine and came to play
But when I took him home he had become
Just like his father. Jointly they would pray
For going back, leaving this hostile fen
Where we'd look at them sideways, then, 'Amen'.

Previously Unseen

Small Car Lady Driver

Cars crushed up tightly by the traffic lights,

Intense inspection as they shortly edged

Then shuffled forward, breaking into fights

That almost happened. Still in convoy wedged

But, several moments later, down the street.

A small two-seater slowly floated past,

The driver tall, mature, a lady neat,

Her husband almost hidden by her vast

And upright stance. She held the wheel

In pincer grip, no slip-shod mode

Of navigation. You could almost feel

Her will the car go on along the road,

Her hat festooned with strangely wilting flowers,

Their destination's distance two more hours.

Skip With A Rope

To the car with mother close behind,
Skipping step on step on little beat;
Skipping rope spins round about in time
The little girl with tickles in her feet.
Winding arms make wide the busy path,
Stop and start this skip-along balloon,
While down beneath the ever-sleeping earth,
Inside her mind the silent simple tune.
How will the world ahead spread out the years
For such a girl as this? We cannot know
But now she's so alive that any tears
Dry in the wind before the mood can show.
Her mother walks behind and watches where
She moves with sunshine in her dancing hair.

Previously Unseen

Garden Bicycle

A small child's bike upon the neat front lawn

Thrown down. No children's games around, no play;

The silence butter-spread like mist at dawn,

Content to hang around on holiday.

Where was the child whose bicycle was dropped

Abandoned, rubbished, several hours ago?

Inside the house the speaking had full-stopped,

A sterile time but someone that I know

Walked slowly by and coughed and wiped his face;

His footsteps scraped the gritty concrete ground.

I watched him go. The front door moved; a space

Had opened just a bit and something made a sound.

I waited for a child to claim its prize.

Nobody came. Still over there it lies.

Going Home From School

The hour passed by, the bulk of children left
With parents, friends or making their own way
To homes around the village warp and weft,
To tea-time relaxation and to play.
So quietly flowed the minutes after spent
And shyly local wildlife had returned
To overlook the wide hard path, intent
On echoing the lessons earlier learnt.
Then, all alone and full of infant zest,
A young girl, tiny, uniformed and bold
Strode past me so much later than the rest
Mouthing some song to fight away the cold.
Eyes brightly tired, soon she had disappeared
Indoors and school that day was quickly cleared.

Previously Unseen

Sitting in the window

A portrait fixed and still in simple frame
Beside the path, close to the busy road;
He sits sublime and always looks the same,
For complex cells inside his mind corrode.
He waits in hope that people passing by
Spot him inside, behind the bordered pane
Of strengthened glass. The minutes dance and fly,
The next day like the last, all days the same,
Yet, for a moment, as I see him there,
He quietly promotes a fervent love
We two of us together easy share,
A comradeship nobody can disprove.
A smile, a wave, a thumb up in the sky -
I won't escape this singularity.

Housebound

Rap on her door and she will come to you,
Open it slightly, hesitate some more
To quiz your face, a wondering if you
Are friend or foe tap-tapping on her door.
The looks of such relief when her recall
Clicks in to easy contact, so refined.
Why, nobody can really know at all
That intercourse like that is so confined.
The home all trim and tidy, like herself,
Goods sometimes van-delivered, otherwise
A neighbour kindly gets them, like an elf
Who promises to please, a nice surprise.
And yet a prison could no stronger be
Than this home where she wanders, slightly free.

Previously Unseen

Scrap Metal Collector

A wiry lad, real smile upon his face,
Knocked firmly at the door to ask if we
Had anything of metal at our place
That he might take, that he could have for free.
I sensed that he'd been threatened, turned aside
By persons everywhere he tried his pitch
But felt he was a worker, had some pride,
Even though his trade would never make him rich.
Could I be wrong? He loaded up his truck
And passed the time of day in fellowship
So when he left I wished him lots of luck
And hoped that he would profit from his trip.
The battered fridge and heater that he had
We didn't want – I'm sure he's not that bad.

Shop Keeper

Looking through the cloudy window glass
From a comfortable wooden seat,
Watching all the local traffic pass
The traffic lights that orchestrate the street,
He, like a Buddha, meditates on life,
Its richness as it runs its road to death.
No customers inside his shop; a knife
Might interrupt his comfortable breath;
A terrorist from distant foreign lands
With frenzied eyes might throw him to the floor
Then run, on fire, dark murder in his hands.
He wakes, he stands; he stares beyond the door,
Beyond the sunlit morning of the world,
The magic of the new day now unfurled.

Previously Unseen

Ice Cream Seller

His van is parked beside the path for hours,

Through summer's sun and mild-spun breezes while

Both young and old with blue sky-building flowers

He threads around his bright-white ice cream smile.

Come here, you happy people, queue along

Beside the van and you will smoothly gleam

Through finest, warmest days, his cooing song

In union with your favourite ice cream.

Nothing there can take away the thought

He has within his organizing brain

That every cone or flake that you have bought

Brings pounds and pennies to him just the same.

Oh, do not judge his purpose is to get

More money, for he casts a tasty net.

Lady with a following Dog

The dark-eyed dog with long and pointed ears
Is known to always follow, magnetised
By leading lady, till she disappears.
It senses this and seems not too surprised
When she goes into shops; it sits by doors
Through which it stares, unblinking, silent, still.
A cup of coffee, sofa, wooden floors,
Newspapers close at hand, later the bill,
Followed by some reluctance to emerge
And reunite with her companion.
Emotion they both feel, a minor surge,
Before they step the street and then are gone.
No witnessed signal shows their curious love;
They fit together, hand in paw - or glove.

Previously Unseen

Man in a Boat

'How great the need to see the way ahead

Whenever passengers depend on you,'

His face conveyed; the things he said,

The safety of the passengers he knew

Were foremost in his mind each journey's length.

He sold boat seats for tourists to enjoy

His tried, unrivalled navigational strength.

The river always praised this river boy

But was he tested by its deepest part

As up and down the gentle stream he steered

So easily? No fear swirled in his heart,

No challenges upset his mature years,

Suggested that he sell his tourist boat,

But when he did he felt alive, afloat.

Man with Bad Leg

He came towards me slowly down the path
Walking with a most peculiar gait.
In other circumstances I might laugh
But this time I knew I ought to wait.
About sixty, his coat a dingy grey,
He struggled past me, rather slow his pace,
Now hunched and shuffling; nothing I might say
Would take away submission from his face.
What had done this? What had made him slack?
Had there been an accident, a fall
To make his body crumple like a stack
When, years and years ago, he'd been quite tall?
His look was just like mine in many ways,
Because we'd shared the air all of our days.

Previously Unseen

Mobility Scooter Lady

I can't be certain what caused her to need
To get about on four electric wheels,
To ride the city range on such a steed
Instead of platform shoes or red high heels.
In such a hurry, cornering so fast,
Hunched up, wrapped up and staring down below
As if today, light, dry and overcast,
Will be the final one she'll ever know.
Most likely, then, her time is desperate,
And illness rushes deep within her veins.
May every moment count before, too late,
She's cornered by her final moment's pains.
No wonder, then, she smokes for all she's worth
Before her smoking spirit leaves this earth.

Young Lady on a Bus

Her eyebrows told a life in happiness;
For thirty years a slender, mindful bough
Of mother's tree; a look of tenderness
As perfect as I see in her face now.
No need to speak it, need to be explained
Why she promote her every waking move
To some chaotic world; her words restrained
Burst out from deep within as hopeful love.
But as I contemplate her simple look,
Her smile, those eyebrows' arched magnificence,
I wonder if she is an open book
Or does she smile to hide indifference?
A second glance: her ever-graceful smile
Convinces me that she is without guile.

Previously Unseen

A Priest without Pride

His glasses clear, worn without metal rim,
His black suit shiny, old and done,
So many days since he had first met sin,
Confessions uttered, absolutions won.
The poorest, an example to his peers,
A heart of iron and a heart of life,
Smooth-faced; though old, so young for all his years;
A practiced giver, sink for others' strife.
Sworn principles the rock on which he stood
Made plenty witness to his faith's ideal;
No earthly pain, no pressure against good
Could easily divert him; his appeal
One step beyond the priesthood's mission line.
He was a very special friend of mine.

Agency Nurse

A speeding car drew up and she got out
To sniff the air and patter through the clutch
Of sheltered houses, like a roundabout
With tenants rabbits in a rabbit hutch.
Consulting with her notes, she's visiting
A small selection of that station's halt.
She knocks on doors or sometimes bells she'll ring,
Forced smile as residents draw back a bolt.
Apologising for her visits then
And swiftly to assess a tenant's need;
Goodbyes, another knock, another den
As she aims to complete the final deed;
Back to the car, notes scribbled, then the key
Turned in the starter – Didn't visit me.

Previously Unseen

Wrinkles

This mirror must have faults; it isn't fair,
Accentuating details not desired.
No streaks of flesh, no white declining hair
On me till it in spitefulness conspired
To indicate those spotted wrinkled hands,
The sags, the bags, the wheeze. The constant frown
Impedes my image though I smartly stand
And slope in modern dress around the town.
Should it be sold or thrown into a skip?
Nothing will make me gaze in it again
For I have noticed that it tends to grip
Upon what's very slightly under strain.
There, out the door, you wretched glass buffoon
And you must stay there; keep out of my room!

Olives

Sells olives on a weekly market stall,
Variety the spice of life writ large.
On her bright face, her challenge to us all
To buy a tub, so modest is the charge.
I might consider doing so one day
When life is dull and nothing's on the boil
But something in her smile keeps me away
From samples of her luscious fruit, the oil.
She stands almost to attention, though can seem
To manifest in person hidden wares;
One casual blink and you slip down a dream
That she has spun to catch you unawares.
So do not let yourself be taken in;
This olive seller gets beneath your skin.

Previously Unseen

Horticultural Assistant

The lanky lad needed to earn his keep;
The College grounds were not how they should be,
Untidy, piles of rubbish, heap on heap;
A chance he might improve, a lottery.
For never had this young man been employed,
So recently a student of the place.
He was a steady learner: he enjoyed
The sights, the smells, the tasks, the gentle pace.
All lawns and hedges, pot plants, ponds and trees
Became this growing gardener's domain.
His efforts were appreciated, pleased
The eye; like royalty he reigned.
The years progressed, he left to go elsewhere
But still I see bright flowers in his hair.

On Mummy's Knee

The push-chair is collapsed and pulled up close

To where she's parked herself upon the seat,

The baby lowered on her knee to doze,

Mother and child, a union complete.

The baby, grappled up to this new place,

Alert, avoiding sleep, stares at the sky,

Especially at any unknown face

On anybody walking up and by.

Not really expecting some surprise,

The mother catches up on her own time;

The baby spots my own approaching eyes

And penetrating glances throws at mine.

We share a momentary love affair;

The mother wakes and I'm no longer there.

Previously Unseen

Home Worker

A daily duty, to be kind to all,

Not grumble, scatter insults on the dust,

Not push people away, not ever call

Them names - Do everything we said you must.

For many years he swept the garden path,

In winter scattered salt, moved things around,

Changed light bulbs, fixed the shower and the bath:

No worker quite like him was ever found.

How was it that he always did all this,

And more besides, when he so wanted to

See all the world? Such dreams of thwarted bliss,

Stuck here inside old timers' final zoo.

Maybe he was afraid of what he'd find

Out there which might distress his cosy mind?

Ornithologist

The gentle hiss of seashore sand and reeds

Makes soporific mindsets spread into

The silent sleuths who hold to simple creeds

Concerning observations, how to do

The things that ornithology holds dear;

The looking, checking from extensive lists

The names and natures of the birds they hear

And see. The morning off-shore breeze or mists

Lull him into a frozen, sculptured pose,

With telescope and tripod hauled about

To set up quickly, make the distance close

Bring wild birds' wonders, colour, flight and shout

To cause his young heart flutter recognition,

And to his species list, one more addition.

Previously Unseen

Pony and Trap Man

He played, so I was told ages ago,

A wealthy farming gent in tweed attire,

Feared by his men who looked up from below

As he drove in his trap, his eyes cold fire,

Ambitious to arrive with least delay

Outside the old hotel with darkened rooms,

With hidden corners, private, one might say,

Where small groups met and spoke in secret tones.

Like a stranger from a distant town

He swings the door to stare, find men he knows.

A sudden quiet draws across his frown

As the door shuts and some acclaim his pose.

They say I used to wave as he drove by

And he waved back where childhood met his eye.

Reader

In any public library you will find
A scramble for the news in papers new,
Soon rather wrinkled, shuffled, undermined
By scruffy men who read them through and through
In detail, more than editors expect
From people on the early morning train,
Who sit in grandeur, millionaires-elect,
Off to the city, finance on the brain.
The trains stop. Readers in them clamber out
Leaving behind 'The Times', 'The Daily Mail'
For others on the mirrored journey. Stout
Library readers concentrate, prevail
Till closing time is imminent and then
They leave; tomorrow they'll be back again.

Previously Unseen

Ancient Cyclist

Perhaps one day I'll be like him, the gent

I saw come trundling down the car-lined street,

Old bicycle, old mac, old legs, content

To circulate the town from on its seat.

Complete, but how can anybody guess

The changes that he might have had to make

To stay alive and well? One can but stress

The several chances that he had to take;

Some wartime dangers surely buffeted,

The illnesses he'd had and long endured,

A workload dull and in some factory shed,

Age fighting boldly back and visions blurred.

He slowly, slowly passed and disappeared.

The winter sun came out, the day had cleared.

Wellington Boots

Back in the times when I worked on the land
The wellingtons we used all oddly squeaked
Of slush whenever dampness was at hand
But mine seldom, if ever, split and leaked.
This all came back to me as he, dog led,
Marched heavily with giant's relentless strides
Into the future. Those before him fled
Or side-stepped clumsily. He onward rides
With home and chocolate biscuit waiting there,
Soft fleece-lined slippers and a warming stove,
A nestling in a comfortable chair,
And open hearth reflecting heat that glows
Unlike the winter's melancholic nip.
His rubber boots are drying, drip by drip.

Previously Unseen

Waiting

Waiting in the waiting room, the dark
And rainy early evening looking in,
The two of us were woken with a start -
The quiet sliding door. Her form, not trim,
Belonging to a lady sewn too close
So tense restricted in her general walk.
She glided to a bench with token pose,
A paperback precluding any talk
Or smile or common thought that might arise,
Communicating something with us there,
Permit a look into another's eyes,
Spin aspects of this place to simply share
The moment. Soon she'd changed her flurried mind,
Stood, walked away and left us both behind.

Assistant

A face with jolly shine and slimy eyes

Smiles at the customers who, through the door,

Search on the shelves to find the special prize

That's somewhere, an antique worth fighting for.

He doesn't know much detail but extends

An aura of strong confidence that rolls

Down corridors of furniture; pretends

A background in oil paintings, ancient dolls,

Toy cars, pith helmets, silky eastern hats.

There's much to see. The customers have gone

And he is left to chortle with the chaps

About his mum, the telly, anyone

Who comes to buy a wonderful antique,

Then sent to check the radiator's leak.

Previously Unseen

Tyre Fitter

He was, I like to think, a normal man,
Stretched out inside the garage office room,
Reading a paper till the clock began
To show the shift was ending very soon.
He did agree the job would not be fun
But needed doing and the fairest price
So, next day came and shortly after one
I went to see if he had the device.
Assured, then fitted with but short delay,
He sauntered deep inside his cosy pit.
The bill described and soon to go away,
Last moments all composed of backing it
And grateful signals, thanking him once more
For putting straight the bent bit of my door.

Bad Feet

Some elementary slow feet don't alert
A traveller along the road to anywhere
But his were awkward; shoes encased in dirt,
Stepped slowly, waving, long-time in the air.
A lack of shave yet no excess of beard,
Limp shoulders sought to pull him all along;
I knew that, though he looked a little weird,
This was because his feet weren't very strong.
Later I couldn't help but watch his trail
Along the shops until close up he stared
Through steamed-up glass; pathetic, trapped and frail,
All of him spoke to me that no-one cared.
In retrospect, I should have somehow tried
To speak; he looked so desolate inside.

Previously Unseen

Two on a Wall, Sitting

None sadder-looking, they slouched on the stones,
Close to the proudly-seated cathedral's door.
Both anthems to our modern youth, their bones
Wrapped close with flesh, their hating faces saw
A future bright with burnt-out stolen cars
Down muddy lanes where no-one ever goes
Disturb the sky, extinguishing the stars.
Rolled cigarettes and hoods fill up their pose;
One might have been a brooding infant, hit
More than a little by a father's fist,
The other broken, losing bit by bit
The bonding with the mother that he missed.
Both guesses, so should I sit there instead
Because my smugness cancels all I've said?

Blotched Look

Just there the taxis glide and slowly park

And passengers arrange a destination

Like prostitutes assembling in the dark

Awaiting their connections, not the station.

A statuary figure there presided,

While cars were all away on booked intent,

A noble man whose purpose seemed divided

Between a taxi ride and some event

Where dancing girls and wine were his possession,

Sought hiding in a dustbin near at hand

Where nobody could witness the impression

Of ugliness he towed across the land.

He didn't move away while I was there

Nor did I see him glance at ladies' hair.

Previously Unseen

Brightly Clad Lady

A spitting sky near where the bus would pass,
A battering north-east wind one afternoon,
Arms folded tightly, fingers cold as glass
And dark eyes quivering in the clouds' low gloom.
I saw that image, saw her waiting there,
An eastern lady, warm as summer days,
Speak to a carpenter who took some care
Explaining to her down-cast, dark-eyed gaze
That she, though not a lady of this part,
Would feel more welcomed, more content,
Should he, an honest man, with red-blood heart,
A castle build, so that she'd soon consent
To be his wife. I know this tale is true;
You were the princess, I built it for you.

Two Miles Away

A young man with a far-connected name,
Across the fields, his home behind the trees,
Lived ordinarily, a certain frame
Made easy as he put the world at ease.
Always I found him open and sincere,
A friendly, normal person, confident,
A visitor for almost half a year,
A proper man with being simply meant.
Then he was gone; his haunts, his mysteries,
Those finer moves were lost from here, a block
Not in its place, cut off, no fine degrees,
No minute-marking check on constant clock.
In fact, I missed his clear companionship,
His morning sun, his hand in careless grip.

Previously Unseen

Three Dogs

I do see how it is, in Arctic lands

Where livelihoods are tempered by the snow,

That several dogs are several willing hands

To pull your sledge and take you where you go.

But in this lovely country, temperate,

With neither cold nor heat to challenge us,

Why have a flock of dogs to contemplate

When travel is by foot, by car, by bus?

He doesn't need to have that canine tribe,

That trio, tied to him, along the street.

It makes me grin to see him boldly stride

And watch his posse strangely incomplete;

Where is the sledge on which his double sits?

I guess it's in his garage all in bits.

By the Shop Window

Stalls abandoned, sellers packed and gone,
The market-place a bomb-site leaking sound,
Abandoned shoppers, finished with their fun,
With aching feet go off across the town.
A frightened man in dirty clothes parades
Close to one shop on market day all year.
He stands by that shop window which displays
Shop dummies which, like him, try to appear
Looked at and spoken to, yet spurned by those
Who spot the questions such strange bodies bring,
A turbulence that skews the human pose
That forms them, blurs the drama that they sing.
Yes, turn aside from him, go home and thank
The Lord you've got some money in the bank.

Previously Unseen

Child in a car

The traffic lights, cars pause and slouch on by;

Lights change, another stream goes on and straight.

A big car stops; the driver wonders why

Right turning is prevented and must wait.

This inactivity, as if to breathe down deep,

While driver looks to slip quickly across,

Gives moments for a well-wrapped child, near sleep,

A front-seat passenger, its mind at loss,

Interrogate my space. A moment new,

Its body rose, as if to leap up high

While I gazed at it, burst the window through

As if we'd met and cried an ancient cry.

Too soon the traffic made its passageway;

Our friendship had to wait another day.

The Observer

With jowls like that to complement the rest,
Big glasses, likewise hat, neat clothes to fit
A short and rounded body made to test,
To see if he might make much sense of it,
The whole of life, the trickle and the flood,
The going-on, excesses and the slack,
The leap to bad, the quiet walk to good.
He sees me look, I'm sure, then turns his back,
Makes out-of-sight adjustments to his gaze,
Then clear sight lines in order to compare
Their means, their health, their skills, their days,
Society and solitude laid bare.
We are as one in our projected schemes
As well as in the minor in-betweens.

Previously Unseen

Taxi Driver

Hard to see his head, a little chap

Who drives a taxi, old, dark and austere.

Eyes like mice, keeps peering through the gap,

Mekon-like; he's done this many-a-year.

Never one to scoop up toffees, fags,

Or lounge with mates beside the station halt,

Uncanny man, helps ladies load their bags

Yet brakes so hard it gives his load a jolt

That makes their nodding heads dip down and back,

Their round-eyed eyes now very like his own.

He, happy with his inconsistency, his lack

Of style, goes steaming through the watching town.

He's safe? I'm nervous, wouldn't bet my cash -

Those eyes, you know, so small, so sharp, so flash.

Dark Glasses

Dark glasses on a down-turned tiny nose,
Iron eyes, black-tinted, immobile;
Planted boots, black lace-ups, candid pose,
He stands behind his bike without a smile.
Nobody passes where he stands to speak
To him today, to make him want to be
A pleasant person, for he is a freak,
Without an urge to move and to be free.
What does it mean to scorn this sorry brother?
His missing sense had never charmed his home.
He never could become a special lover
For people such as he can only roam
Into the leaves, the leaves that ever spread
Around where simple people seldom tread.

Previously Unseen

Dead Ducks

How green the field in front of the cathedral,
The leafy walks criss-crossing, cool to foot,
An open space uncluttered, breath for people
Who make the most of gaps; I choose to cut
Through to the car park, face the going home
With shopping bag and empty thinking, yet
A look to the side inspires a dissonant groan;
Alone, without a life to call a pet,
She's sitting low down on a battered seat,
With bulging eyes and plastic bag of bread,
Intending to reward the ducks, a treat.
With words she wooed, the words inside her head;
'Come here, my friends, eat up, this manna's gold.'
Bread's poison for a duck, I have been told.

Spirit buyer

A check-out line, a place of thought and calm
For me, at least, but he was flustered, tall,
A thinly-built stick insect lacking charm
Who'd lately left the bridge in a long fall.
I've jumped ahead, sense manic, latent fear
Watching, watching, as he tried to go
With bottle of cheap whiskey, disappear,
Soon from the bridge a mutilating throw.
Follow and save him when he advertised
The awful moment, seconds from no more?
He took his change and looked a bit surprised
To find himself outside the open door.
Inert, I stood and watched and watched him leave;
I didn't know him - How was I to grieve?

Previously Unseen

Fear

This country has a lot to answer for
And yet we're seldom prone to real fear
That stacks up in our hearts till evermore,
At any moment, any time of year.
He seemed to hug the buildings, no small stake
In bricks to strangle or shoot in the back;
He knows the crowd about all want to make
A trap to catch a person, have a knack
Of evil retribution; no way out
For him, the only man contained in hell.
Should he break cover, run along without
Much hope of finding daylight in his cell
I 'm sure he'd be tripped up and, on his face,
Admit the measure of his one disgrace.

Slim, Long Hair

So like a sapling tree, at eight or nine

A skipping little person, trimmed to be

Later in life a magnet, to combine

Soft love with action, all yet early, free

From puzzlement and failed affections that

Set traps to trip and tumble to the floor.

Oh, what a time in life to waltz about

The safest places, to be heading for

The harbour's furthest point! I could espy

The ship she'll sail in not be turned aside

But stream in lines of spray below the sky,

To sit within the fiercest winds, beside

Time's spring. She could not understand

Wild things would happen, being planned.

Previously Unseen

Furrowed Forehead

No sign, no sign of anything amiss,
A comfortable step, an upright back
But lines all on her face had scored out bliss
And prompted fields of never living black
Or maybe even sin, a painful soul;
So many images wrapped tightly around
The headlines that were almost darkly told
About the causes of her open wound.
She splashed her look on every person near,
A challenge to their armies to explain
To her some reason for her primal fear,
A purpose to her elemental pain.
But nothing penetrated; nothing said
It was the answer to her aching head.

Shop Front

The opening day presented passers-by
A chance to see the shop was really there.
Inside, the owner came to wonder why
She'd bothered setting up for those who stare
And don't come in to find that goods displayed
Are bargains, necessary, so refined
That none can do without them. Early trade
Was limited, not what she had in mind.
Door opens, such relief, a rescue bold,
A search to see what offers in the store
Might tantalize, might even now be sold.
No, they begin retreating to the door,
Smile, nod and indicate that they must go.
All's well: delightful things remain on show.

Previously Unseen

Hair In Waves

His buttoned coat was fawn, gloves held his hands,

His striking hair the waves of southern seas,

His distant look the scent of foreign lands

That long ago had forced him to his knees.

There are strange tales in him that should be told,

Adventures wonderful, of hope, of fear;

How he had come across a pot of gold,

How something made it slowly disappear.

Like people everywhere, he'd dreamed a dream;

Success the rock on which we want to lie.

We ride beneath the ever-swirling stream

Yet chances coming to us go on by.

More beckon so we scramble up again,

Ignore the stop-sign, miss the speeding train.

Lady Musing

Black jacket, short, high heels and angled hat,
A clipped stiff walk, small parcel held up close,
An ordinary face but after that
No more to tell. However, I suppose
She might have been in trouble, overcome
By fears of what solution he'd contrive,
What challenge to her person, what be done
To shake out her condition, open eyes
Now inwardly intense and locked upon
Her understanding that he'd find her out;
Her status then a wretched, tuneless song,
Though that's a battered suitcase full of doubt.
Come, lady, make the sun come out, to flame,
To make you smile, get him do the same.

Previously Unseen

Long-Coated Lady

Her daughter had a daughter who was cruel,
Who lied and stole and broke the young men's hearts
For miles around. Some cried, some fought a duel
While others plunged below the watermarks.
No wonder that her face betrayed her fears
As down the street she wrapped herself around
Such trials that she'd endured for many years.
Harsh looks from others; soon she would be found
On horseback, off to northern forest lands
Where frosted gales strike craggy mountain sides,
Where short green grass by dunes gives way to sands
And waves like mountains parry gentle tides.
None of this matters to her. All I said
Remains a story deep inside my head.

Melodeon Man

A glimmered memory of another time
Back then, when sun shone, breezes blew and we
Made merry in our younger, days-past prime
With friends of many kinds who might not be
The most athletic dancers. But we tried
To call up a performance fit to watch.
He played to raise a spirit from inside
Our simple souls and upwards snatch
Our anchored bodies, take the Morris cry
And fling it up the sunny Suffolk air,
Yet reticent to flout his skills, so shy
That he could be unseen, were he not there.
Oh, how we loved to dance, to add our soul
To all his music making, make it whole!

Previously Unseen

Newspaper Man

He must have swallowed something very hot,

A bottle filled with firewater, for

In winter, he in shorts, easy to spot,

Delivers local papers door-to-door.

Of course, it would have come as no surprise

Had he been in his twenties, thereabouts,

But he's considered old; his grizzled eyes

And blotch-backed hands erasing any doubts

Concerning his great age. So what's the game,

Why under-dress in rainy, slushy streets

When others wrap around, appear the same?

He looks at all the people that he meets

But moments never seem to come along

For him to share his warmth, burst into song.

Young Man in a Public House

The door opened. Inside, in the warm,
A noisy crowd shared hopes and memories,
The day's concerns, the van, the sport, the storm;
No doubt this was a time to take my ease.
When I'd been there awhile and sipped my beer,
Seen men I knew from many years before,
I saw a figure standing over there
On guard, protect his spot upon the floor,
For though he seemed part of the raffish throng
Enjoying all the banter of the night,
I watched him think their posturing was wrong
Within the pub's day-consuming light.
This was the chain that linked to his childhood
When mummy told him how he must be good.

Previously Unseen

A mobile phone

His mobile phone on crooked arm to ear,
His voice that stuttered in the Suffolk town,
One-sided conversation's rage would disappear,
No small attempt to keep the volume down.
In natty jeans and jacket, not a tie,
Face deadly, frosty; every thought concealed
Except this wordy waterfall come sweeping by
In public, conversation part-revealed.
I did not want to know the deal he made,
His frown, his smile, success he dramatised.
Why must he share this stuff so overplayed
To swamp the afternoon I idolised?
Just then he walked towards the big hotel.
The sun still shone, I blinked and all was well.

On Every Road

On every road and on and on he went,
Tracking down a line, a winding trail,
Pinioned eyes always appeared intent,
Bicycle the transport of this snail.
How old was he? I really couldn't tell
Because each year he'd never seemed to change,
Wore the same clothes that suited him that well
And within limits wheeled and wheeled a range.
He knew he really didn't own this world:
He lived alone, just on the edge of town.
What made him self-contained, so inward-furled,
His cosy pedals turning round and round?
I called his name as he went slowly on:
He simply smiled and in a trice was gone.

Previously Unseen

Aglow

The unavoidable, infectious mist
Hands out its greasy, mealy punishment
To batter down the places on its list,
Complete control, mysterious intent.
Then along he comes, a strange-eyed man,
His face aflame with silvered energy,
Makes men and women wonder if he can
Hold back, turn back this foggy, foggy sea.
He wasn't known round here; a lovely soul,
Till weather wrapped him up in rusted chains.
Now, with his warmth he turns around the cold
Damp sky and strangers long-worn weathered
pains.
The children asked him if his skill is found
All over, not just slipping, sliding round.

Old Lady, Shopping Trolley

Old lady, shopping trolley hunting down
In well-stocked supermarket; bread and cakes
And wine and sandwiches, the best in town
It's said. Small jars of chutney she still makes
And scrawls on stick-on labels all the same,
Avoiding much confusion later on
When looking for replacements. She is lame
And walks about with awkward steps upon
The big shop floor. She searches all around,
Pulls up her gloves, adjusts her blue beret
But nowhere is a trolley to be found:
She wanders off and soon has gone away.
Later I see her peering round again
With empty bags and beret still the same.

Previously Unseen

House to Let

So close, a van, behind its open door
Had been parked up, ramp sloping down, askew
With furniture, a freezer, not before
Into the open air since purchased new.
He wheeled the sack truck from his 'Just Sold'
home,
More clutter for the huge removal van,
Apologised for taking up the room
And blocking up the path. The little man,
With curly hair and ordinary face
And ordinary clothes and busy smile,
Where was he going, why was he displaced?
That old house had a most attractive style;
Could it just be he felt it overmuch,
Ashamed he had a coarse and common touch?

Only A Farmer

From end to end across the field he goes
Into the wind then back and once again,
His tractor ploughs and cultivates and hoes,
Whatever weather comes, the sun, the rain.
Only a farmer knows the loneliness
Of open fenland, black and blown and raw,
That challenges, that you can never guess
What harmful consequence spreads out before.
He hasn't special skills, far less the cash
To cope with crop rotation, fair and square;
Sometimes his judgement verges close to rash,
Crops fail, the market isn't even there.
This son of toil is active, wild and brave
And fenland soil will serve him as his grave.

Previously Unseen

Poser

Once, years ago, when he was young and free,
His days of sun and rain were still to come.
You get the message – He is history,
The future, past, today all in him one.
His uniform eccentric, actions strange,
The empire of the world his fingertips,
A European rider on the range,
To left and right a kiss close to his lips.
Now doubts and puzzles scratch to get within
His spirit-crackling lively character,
Come creeping nearer, serpent-like and thin
To pierce his rusting armour and to stir
His sediment deep down, to tie his hand
Stop him from wandering about the land.

Saxophonist

I knew his music and his easy skills
From many years ago, thought him long gone
From this small town into the eastern hills
To re-form his rock band but I was wrong.
He stayed and soon built up a steady trade
In sheet music, old instruments, repairs,
Whilst bookings for the music that he played
Came now and then to catch him unawares.
He found this situation suited best,
His character so mole-like: he agreed
He needed stillness so that he could rest
Inside his low-lit dusty shop, his creed
Not changed from cool days of our muddy youth
When we believed our music spoke the truth.

Previously Unseen

In the Charity Shop

So small a shop, so loud a trenchant voice,
No chance for echoes; coats and china, books
Absorb her growls, a buyer's choice
No mitigating angry, taunting looks.
She can't appreciate the finer styles,
The well-worn boots, the off-white vest,
Teak cabinet or ever-growing piles
Of cast-offs. She herself is hardly dressed
To sell to shoppers novel, inspired use
Of pewter jugs or lidless teapots bright.
Her tone of speaking almost seems abuse;
She'd rather book a ticket, take a flight
To sun-cooked islands, sleep upon the beach
Just anywhere where she'd be out of reach.

In The Doctor's Waiting Room

On comfortable seat and on her own
She sits, nursing her necessary stick.
It's clear she's worried, sitting all alone;
You cannot tell she may be very sick
Except that on her face her oaken stare
Is fixed. She has those non-committal eyes
'Might it be my heart or something rare,
A growth, the brain, I don't know what.' She sighs,
'It isn't fair!' I hear her silent shout
Rebound across the empty waiting room
And ricochet in echoes all about
This place that'd witnessed many cries of gloom.
I see what's been her mindset all this year
In trying to hide the measure of her fear.

Previously Unseen

Jogger

Legs pumping at a most convincing rate,
Co-ordinating arms a swirl of steel,
A track suit purchased at an early date,
Matched running shoes now slightly down-at-heel.
No heart-rate monitor, no bright headband,
For this is just a Sunday morning's run
And budding athletes like him in this land
Imagine pain-for-fitness signals fun.
I knew him well but now he will not grin
As we meet on the path we often share.
Why can't he look into my face, begin
To let past quarrels go and clear the air?
I sense there'll be no handshake as we pass:
I see him coming, step upon the grass.

Background

I have a plan, to never to be seen,

Stay out of sight, blend in, slide by the wall,

Do such that, even if I maybe scream

My vacancy may keep my presence small.

Try this, you people stumbling through the day,

To stop and sense where might be my domain

And point your fingers at me right away;

I promise you that I will not complain.

Evaluating what affect my speech

Made on them, I was smartly thrown aside,

For not a single person in my reach

Bothered to take me up, even deride

Me for my well-planned empty strategy.

In consequence, I soaked in apathy.

Previously Unseen

Unnoticed

I did not see him when I moved away
To drive a mile or two to home, the fire,
My mission to undo the routine day.
Will something help me climb out of the mire?
Another quarter mile and still no sign
Of him, his hands in pockets, simple stroll
Behind me, all a rubbed out, done-for line
Diminishing in space and time and soul.
The mirror doesn't lie but may play tricks
Confuse or even alter what may be
And in it there, an image of him sticks,
Not lost but on the move: I think it's me,
For anyone we meet is what we are
And so is he. I stop, reverse the car.

Two Polystyrene Coffee Cups

A smouldering cigarette in woollen glove,
A distinct, scoured face and light-rinsed hair;
High heels make her squint to look above
The swaying row of passing shoppers there.
Why did she hold two coffee cups? Had he
Not understood the hour nor her heart,
Not realised she needed company?
Slipped footsteps in the street; she stood apart.
I turned a corner, down a narrow path,
Forgot that I had watched her wide-eyed face,
Her solid sadness and her silent laugh
Despair for his returning to her place.
Is she there now, her arm still holding up
Cold coffee in one polystyrene cup?

Previously Unseen

Be Gone

Whenever smiles striped lines across his face,

His eyes hid deep beneath his common grind,

The morning dew a signal of the grace

That covered all his moments of his mind.

For if you saw somebody going by

Aghast with unimaginable love

You nearly always knew the reason why;

That they had met the person from above.

Can it be true; can people who we see

Be influenced by someone who seems wise,

Who spends his churning life in harmony,

With distant death so close before his eyes?

I don't know, but when he has been around,

I think, today, tomorrow can't be found.

Thin Young Man

A momentary glance, so all-alive,
Across the road before the next car came,
Slipping through the shoppers, twenty-five,
One destination. He might not explain
Why, just avoiding people passing near
Like woven thread, compact and singular,
As slender as a willow's wand, he'd steer
Himself to meet some princess from afar.
I say 'afar', but this must be revealed;
The distances involved are local, as the crow
Flies for a while then settles on a field
Close by, slow glides and stands on earth below.
So focussed was he on his special one,
Expected that she must be there, not gone.

Previously Unseen

Restaurant Assistant

The evening shift so busy, all the staff
Strode through the restaurant as on skis,
No time to stop, no time to have a laugh,
Express their hurts or their anxieties.
She asked us in, soon put us at our ease
With little kindnesses that we could tell
Were more than in her remit, just to please,
To make us really happy; she was swell.
Time for a meal with friends and then goodbye,
A tip as usual left upon the plate.
Your look said paid-up thanks; I caught your eye
And spoke to you with a smile to indicate
My gratitude, more than one might expect,
Surprised you then by being so direct.

Tennis Player

Each Saturday a summer's tennis day,
In whites well-pressed the tennis court to hire,
In local leagues his sporting pride display
With racket skills well-known throughout the shire;
Hair brushed in place and face a ruddy glow,
Shoes made immaculate, jacket pristine;
The knocking up always a splendid show,
Adjust the net, the grass forever green.
So on and on throughout the day's calm heat,
Set after set, match point, the winning smash:
He was the one they all wanted to beat,
Bring down to earth, reduce to pile of ash.
The season's end, the champion still supreme,
Awaiting next year's local tennis scene.

Previously Unseen

Crime Stopper

All day you see him by the open door

Standing, standing, standing near the flowers

While others move about on the shop floor

As he just gathers dust for hours and hours.

I've never seen him question anyone

Nor raise alarm that there has been a theft.

His eyes say that his tedious job's no fun:

He's still there when the parked-up cars have left.

But I believe he thinks help is at hand;

He laughs at us for we don't know about

His dream of some new promised shopping land

Where all the thugs and thieves become devout.

In which case, there would surely be no need

For him to stand and die – He would be freed!

Dispensing

Repeated conversations and prescriptions
Seldom anything exciting anymore,
Her smile as fixed as ever, same descriptions
Of medicines and tablets as before.
How could packing pills away make sunlight
Invade the room awash with sterile things?
How did her colleagues overcome the frostbite
Of doing this forever? Evening brings
The shift to some conclusion; close the hatch
And check and lock and sign out once again
To dream at home of just another batch
Of oddly-named commercial anti-pain
Concoctions. Soon after her arrival at her home,
Speaks words of love to someone on the phone.

Previously Unseen

Swagger

So much is pleasing in his upright walk;
His being glows with joy to be alive.
Meeting some people for a lunchtime talk?
Will there be oysters or sports cars to ride?
See, on his face, a look of light relief,
No backward glance to show he is afraid;
Was he successful as a daylight thief?
Had he just seen his soldier son's parade?
No sooner seen than out of sight and mind
Till later, when I sat and flicked the day,
His face returned to glimmer and to grind
My thoughts and soon his walk came into play.
Still now this swagger I cannot contain,
Irresolute and scratching at my brain.

Slight and Dark

I waited in a queue a little while
Content to watch for movements round about.
There, hardly looking out, no sense of smile,
A short girl stood wrapped up in common doubt.
No, there was nothing strange in her conceit;
She hardly would be noticed in a crowd;
Teenager from her fingers to her feet
As small as modern posture had allowed.
The unconventional matter of her form
(Though really nothing; nothing drew the line)
Made dark-ringed eyes, perfected by a storm
And lights reflected in them to combine
A beauty and a graceful teenage mind
That nowadays are very hard to find.

Previously Unseen

Garage Owner

A rotund person, cars and fuel selling,

Never left the town; his frequent dream,

A pitch new-mown and crowd supporters yelling,

Was to watch his favourite football team.

First Division fixtures focussed by him

Attentive to all scores, all end results.

Times were mixed so will the ball go flying?

The radio's reportage he consults.

Back to the garage – Mondays, early morning

After the lads have lost away from home

Would you catch him docile, slightly yawning,

As happy as a dog with giant bone?

Quite often he'd be in a frightful mood,

Might even shout out something slightly rude!

Hat Lady

My mother, others, told me to be neat,

Dress thoughtfully and always wear clean shoes

To set off jacket, trousers, so your feet

Become included in your general pose.

That way, no-one would think unkind

Intemperate thoughts about your going out.

The little lady's presence, to my mind,

Epitomised such qualities, no doubt,

For, well-assembled in her warm attire

And pacing evenly along, she showed

The world her past attentions were acquired

As suited her to pass along the road.

A look of satisfaction gave all this

An introspective sense of perfect bliss.

Previously Unseen

Selling Shoes

The shop interior was lit with care,
Its aim to show as tempting, shining gold,
New shoes on stands, boots asking you to wear.
All day like that they wait, hope to be sold
But times are hard and shoppers' wallets out
Of stocks of clinking cash turned into use.
The shop girl, trim and tidy, walked about;
None spoke, none smiled, none gave unkind abuse.
Imagine how her minutes, filled with tasks,
Might make her tired but work-wise satisfied.
This small, uncrowded shop where no-one asks
For help means that her days have died.
What does she think about while nothing's done?
I don't expect she has a lot of fun.

Man Outside The Shop

Don't need a paper, do I? 'Course I do!
You must find out whatever's going on,
The politicians ain't no use to you
Nor are the silly blokes that stands upon
Their arrogance to tell peculiar tales
Of this and that about celebrities
And stuff about that chatty Prince of Wales,
Insurance, dole, the cost of beer and cheese.
You see, such news, they spread it all around -
To get you in your guts; that's what I think —
There's nowhere now where truth is to be found.
This country's done; it's almost on the brink.
You just don't get it? All I say is true!
I must be gone — I've got a lot to do.

Previously Unseen

Mill Man

I only met him once and not his voice,

For grinding dust from corn had shot his speech.

True, working in the mill had been his choice,

Though other tasks were quite within his reach.

I climbed the wooden stairs in several parts

Up to the platform of his citadel;

The air white clouds, the cogged machinery starts

Smooth operations in this cereal hell,

Fine whiteness thrown I'd never before seen.

Inside the mill's confinement, proudly tall,

He wiped his hands and pointed out the gleam,

The sacks, the central hoist, the spaces small.

Remains of him, brushed down that stair,

Are fogged by sack dust everywhere.

Zebra Crossing Incident

Waiting for the drivers' kind attention

Beside the shopping street's striped crossing spot

There stood a solitary whose intention

To go across soon as my car could stop.

No other cars in front or close behind

So my smooth slowing down no big surprise.

Immobile, watched him, tried to read his mind

As he stepped forward with two gloomy eyes.

Two aluminium crutches on his arms

Helped swing his hurting body past and gone.

Does anyone caress him, see his charms,

Smile lovingly, sweep clouds from the sun?

I hope that he soon rises from this mess;

No one should be cut off from happiness.

Previously Unseen

A Kind of Politician

For decades a political prisoner, he
Lived quietly within the catchment's net.
A tiny terraced cottage was his see;
He was the left-wing's special party pet.
They say that he pursued the public service,
The votes to pour into the ballot box,
But nothing told of his impressive purpose,
No speeches, letters to the press, no knocks.
His secrecy close wrapping him around
As plated armour offers strong protection;
It kept him safe from any hint or sound
Concerning his soon-doomed re-election.
Rejection was a fierce body-blow
So home he went. In time his pain would go.

Adonis in Trainers

The top example of the male this year,
How elegant, in body how sublime,
Smooth movement, lightly dressed, a trace so clear
Into the future, into all of time.
Assuredly he is primed to make a mark
In commerce, law or something overseas;
Smooth skin, soft smile and, striding through the park,
His parentage speaks foreign refugees.
See, there he goes, and now is out of sight,
A prince in all dimensions to be seen.
But will the bubbled glass, his chosen light,
Craze easily to blur his handsome screen?
Another day, I see him once again
And envy how he advertises men.

Previously Unseen

Writer

Who writes, for heaven's sake, who wants to write,
Flow indistinct and lengthy plots and plant
Within such characters as minds' eyesight
Accepts and understands, as one might want
To be with or to know about? She told me how
She, too, had tried to document the earth,
Engage with people almost real and now
Wanted her tale printed, for it had worth.
How could I give encouragement, say all
Of it spoke well and that she must advance
To publish, to be damned? Her clarion call
Incessant music; she should take a chance.
Her small smile told me she might really try.
The slope began, now for the mountain high.

An Unexpected Meeting

The rain was falling and the street was grey
As people hurried by. A few, like him,
Slipped from the weather, quite content to play
With items in that shop so dull and trim
Which charity aspired to circulate;
Odd items no more wanted generally
To which some people found they could relate
And rummage all about with energy.
We recognised each other straight away,
A shop-soiled pair; we quickly re-engaged
In common interests – Not a lot to say
About our lives and how they'd been arranged.
We paused when what we said was soon complete.
The door was there: I slipped into the street.

Previously Unseen

When Not Working

I asked, 'What is it that you do when you
Are not in work, have time to choose your way?'
A moment's thought; he said, 'So much to do,
I work for Him. I do His work each day.'
This baffled me so I asked if there were
Things such as reading, crafts, a special seat.
All speaking paused; I felt his mind a blur,
But not at all – His joy was to repeat
His mantra so I smiled. I felt his self
Embedded in his ancient, strong belief
That God had lifted him from off some shelf
To spread His word to crook and cheat and thief.
That may be what he does but does he find
That others' spirits leave him left behind?

Passing Through

Another trolley with its feral pile
Aligns with others at the checkout spot
Where sits the checkout lady all the while
On swivel seat to check what you have got.
From right to left she passes, hand to hand,
Each item past the electronic eye
Then puts them on the shelf where you now stand
And then another, till they've all passed by.
Yet when I gaze at what it is she thinks
As, hour by hour, she thus fulfils her shift
There's nothing in her look - She seldom blinks
And wakes up from her purgatorial drift.
O, lady, check this out and you will see
Elsewhere can give you life if you break free!

Previously Unseen

Pouring Rain Lady

The sheeting rain on Saturday complained
About the cheerful Christmas public face
On many. She brushed down her liquid mane
And moved in elegance and young girl's grace.
Behind, her friend seemed almost incomplete,
No strong expression in his masquerading look
But she had lightning in her spirit's feet
As down the crowded winter's way they took
Consideration of their own imprisoned need
As well as giving way to the other's heart.
How do we sense what she might soon concede,
Show kindness to him latent on her part?
Experience might show, whoever sighs,
No showered blessings, only rain-filled skies.

Premature Baby

A handful, that is all she is to hold,
A heartbeat blinking on her scanner's page,
Skin softly promising much more than gold
But early-born and yet to start her age.
Nine months gestation must be fully ended
Before permission for her life to start.
Her mother waits, has many weeks pretended
Childhood's beginning outlined on a chart
Of goings on, days full of what should be
An infant's journal written in the sky.
The waiting train still asks for catch-up. We
Can only look on, watch the prelude fly.
O, little child, will you have all your wits?
I hope so, pray so, loving you to bits.

Previously Unseen

In the Distance – A Horse

So long ago a film, Omar Sharif,
A desert miraged up a man, a horse,
Today, a nip-pinched walk took me beneath
A blue sky close beside a water course.
Across the ditch and at a distant spot
A horse and rider cantered round and round,
Slow, dressage-like, tying a tiny knot,
A mesmerising point, there, on that ground.
Behind, a rainbow by a low white cloud,
Invisible the drops fell far away
Then absent, just as if they had allowed
The pair to fill the kernel of the day.
As if to fall in with this odd event
I froze in wondering what on earth it meant.

Antiques Young Man

Excitement on the Roadshow comes with cash;
All history and craft adds interest.
He, young man with a fringe, was mild, not rash,
A character whose outlook was the test.
He wasn't looking for some oddity,
Some elegance that smashed you in the face,
But loved the drama, wildly shimmering free,
A gleaming icon for the antique race.
Glassware and paintings, any works of art
Astonished his nerve endings, sharpened breath
To surely increase beating in his heart,
Widened his eyes, the opposite of death.
How can the past invade a mind so much?
He has a far from common, adult touch.

Previously Unseen

Well Done

'What ought I to put on so I'll be seen
In company, get everyone to know
My personage reveals the brightest dream,
Inspires the world wherever I may go?
In slightly rural fashion, boots and cape
The whole impression waxed in woodland hues,
I'll be a focal point, make no mistake,
My tweed suit and my leathery country shoes.'
The fashion photo-shoot about to start
Beside the ancient stone-worked city wall,
I may be wrong, but deep within his heart
He didn't want to be like that at all
But would prefer to set his pose aside,
Transform the wasted fortune of his pride.

At the Bank

New to the task with eyes like a pet dog
Wanting so much to please, be number one
But comes across some strange and helpless frog;
The more he tries, the more he's overcome
By customers who deign to turn away
And look towards the large, glass-fronted hatch
Where, in command, from nine-thirty each day,
The usual cashiers sit in formal watch.
Approaching, pleading, seeking recognition,
He tries enticing custom to his side,
Face up to him in certain commendation.
That dream of right importance, simple pride.
For some time he's been missing; months have passed.
His creaking disposition didn't last.

Previously Unseen

W. I. Husband

The gathering of women almost done,
The hour for going home on end-wall clock,
When in he slid, a figure less of fun
Than shades of drying out, the local look.
The room turned round to him no well-groomed head,
He sat up in a plastic modern chair,
Assuming guardianship. Nothing was said;
I sensed nobody noticed he was there.
Hello, a slight-bowed lady met his glance
And glided to where he in silence sat
And whispered to him. Then, as if by chance,
Announced the raffle time, produced the hat.
Tickets were picked and prizes, jam and tea,
Applauded. All departed merrily.

Two Sticks

A Goretex waterproof and pair of sticks
Assist him in his grasp at places new;
Hat pulled down low and short of many tricks
To get him moving, helping him pull through.
Years long before he might have lived the dream,
Sahara sands, the Himalayan heights,
But now just getting to the shops and home
To tea again make up his few delights.
Left, right, keep going on, step one by one,
Be careful crossing, don't take any chance;
Too late to see this journey bathed in fun
In territory rich in wild romance.
Frustration digs away; his memory
Can't be eroded, wants to set him free.

Previously Unseen

Baseball Cap

Night casts its cloud around and stands at ease,
Cars at the roadside cooling slowly down,
Few are about and dark are the chestnut trees
That see below a young man with a frown.
Short for his age and caressed by a nervous smirk,
Looking to stir up his mates in their company,
Pokes at their grins and leads them to follow his work
To eagerly scatter such bitterness into the sea.
When I was young I was small and was nobody's friend,
Teasing and tricking and forever playing the fool,
Nevertheless I knew when the time came to end
My awful behaviour in class and outside the school.
So why is he seldom considerate, kind to another?
Perhaps he's bullied at home by an out-of-work brother.

Tight-lipped

His eyes and lips and look were very thin,
Thin as a string that can be tightly tied,
Hiding in solitude, alone with kin
Who keep themselves pinned down, stay stuck inside.
Once was a soldier, strong for one his rank
When fighting in the desert and the plain
Then worked to sell the mighty steel-clad tank,
Big guns and drones and military plane.
Now that is over, pension-age, but still
The danger comes from those recalling who
Sold weapons to the tyrants, those who kill.
His panic came when strangers came in view.
So am I sorry when he sees a shark?
I am, but selling death switched on the dark.

Previously Unseen

By the Shop Door

'Don't sit there doing nothing, do something!
Go find a friend, a dog, a lady old and dull,
And when you've had your fill of complaining,
Come in and help us make our trolley full.
You sit there like your father, say you're bored,
That nothing here is any use to you
But in this shop so much has all been stored
To keep us going till the week is through.
What's that? You're off to look around,
Find mischief by the lake down at the park?
You're not – I'm telling you that you'll be found
Right here, I say, 'cos soon it will be dark!'
She disappeared. He sat so very still,
Got bored, as youngsters know they often will.

Theatrical Man

The newsagents are where, it seems, he gets
His kicks: he's daily found in chains behind
The counter; papers, sweets and cigarettes
Are plentiful and passers-by can find
A range of slightly-dated, useful stock
To buy with pocket money, small used change,
And go off leaving him in the same spot.
But what he craves is standing on the stage:
His aim, for decades, has been to become
Far greater than amateur theatre's dream,
The local hero, be another one
That Broadway praises. Will his long-term scheme
That gnaws into his heart as he stands bound
Be realised? Well, life is seldom crowned.

Previously Unseen

Caretaker

No one could say that he'd not done his best,
His body over years had seen the sun
And now he had surrendered to the test,
The end-time: his retirement had begun.
He'd tell the listener the past had often been
A gentle meeting of children and of staff;
So many little stories filled the stream,
Some serious, some brought a mild laugh,
Seemed easy, all the banter and the hours.
But there sat in the background secrecy;
Things were not always chocolate and flowers,
Now buried deep within his memory,
So down the corridor where children throng
Bucket and mop once fetched to get along.

The Same Way

You would not think the two of them refined:
Both are exemplars of contemporary ways.
He, with jeans and trainers, stands behind
The toddler in the push-chair, gently lays
His fingers on his baby for a while.
The child pays no attention, waves a hand
To sweep the air in front, conductor style,
Surveying in its view some promised land.
I wondered, as they both looked into time
Had they more than an inkling of the sad,
Russian roulette of life, a sorry crime
If they abused the moments that they had?
Inside I felt a smile as down the path
He pushed the baby home to have its bath.

Previously Unseen

Checkout Angel

Late in December and the afternoon
Queues leaving, going home with plastic bags
Of gewgaws, armed against the winter's gloom,
Dark skies and time that very often drags.
I stood in line, my thoughts a sterile place,
Just wanting to get on, back to my car.
But there she was; the joyful check-out space
Filled by an angel shining from afar.
'Fear not,' she said, 'I seldom dress this style.
The manager is mad, lacks common sense.'
And in a flash I realised her smile
Was genuine, her dress only pretence.
'Have a nice day,' she grinned, 'I'm off to heaven.
My shift ends soon, you see, at half-past seven.'

Cinema

The flight of steps drops to the basement where
Blue paint is peeling close to lights that glow.
The film was ready to begin down there;
Screen adverts brash and loud precede the show.
Like skiers, setting off down scary slopes,
We pause. We pass our tickets to an ape
Demanding proof of purchase, check our hopes
Before we take our seats so we might gape
On action cut and somehow made to seem
A story set in places rare and real.
Unlike the ape-man, we can live the dream
Tonight. But me, I simply stop and steel
My thoughts. I squint, peer back into his eyes,
Unblinking where imagination lies.

Previously Unseen

The End of School

A winter twilight, pavement spread with frost

On which the back-packed lad walked gingerly,

Not wishing to be late. The road he crossed;

Homework his shell, he ambled home for tea,

His days always a parallel life raft,

Of student peers and dad, an invalid.

The classroom chattered like a summer's draught,

The house a withered place where no-one did

Delight in humour, healthy games or tease

Him till the onward growth of youth was tried

And worked to put the family at ease.

No wonder, then, within his room he cried;

Love and contempt came close, caused him to be

Firm groundings for his school and family.

The Drinker

Think anybody knows what he's become?
Strolls down the street towards the general shop,
Controlled footsteps a measure of the gun
Of booze that's made his life to sip and drop,
Made incoherent speech a trade-mark step
That cannot but enhance the way he goes
Into the shop, more alcohol to get,
To drink at home. Why, everybody knows
That, even if he tossed the habit now,
Tomorrow he'd be coming back to buy
More cans, more bottles of this sacred cow.
An undercurrent spies a time passed by
When he could mould and bend society.
He's now becalmed, a silenced entity.

Previously Unseen

The Big Screen

To the high side of the market wall
The big screen shows the rugby, black and red.
I stand and stare. A player kicks the ball
That should go into touch but drops instead
Into the open, to the clutching grip
Of a young and dark-skinned running man
Who, with a darting, weaving, dancing skip
Goes on to score. I am a rugby fan;
Next to me stood another looking up
To watch the self-same rugby overhead,
Excited by this year's Six Nations Cup,
Just like me. I turned to speak and said,
'You are attracted by this sport, I guess?'
He turned his face to me: it indicated 'Yes.'

Crew-cut Lady

Not to hear her voice was no upset;
I knew her from her face, her calendar
Of all her days gone by, the parapet
That had become the blueprint of her star.
Short hair might mean an illness in the past
But I suspected she had challenged style,
Felt comfortable in putting fashion last;
Inevitable breaches made her smile
And that - her powered grin - was what had pleased
The lych-gate of her worldly-wild success.
Though rivers chased the water to the seas
She'd stood upon a pain of emptiness
And now that drift had eased her foundered craft
I knew the reason why she always laughed.

Previously Unseen

Tall On high Heels

I see myself in clouds of pink champagne,
In conversation stirred by elegance.
Small groups conform in style, declaim
Behind tall stately windows' inward glance.
He doesn't understand my need for grand
And overt sentimental attitude;
High social status to be mine I've planned
But he's so satisfied with solitude.
Rebellious, I have planned my strategy,
One which I know he deems to be extreme,
For even though he's not as tall as me
My new high-heels might propagate my dream.
Together to the city we will go,
Me taller than before, him far below.

Dead Shop Lady

The shop closed up, the stock all gone in store,
A coat of shadow paint gently applied,
A new and subtle sign above the door,
An outlet for dispatching those who'd died.
In well-pressed suit, the lady sat in state
Awaited clientele related to
Whoever was no more, the so-called 'late',
To organise the crematorial 'do'.
However, each time that I passed the door
Reluctance had kept everyone at bay:
She looked so slighted and so slightly sore
That people should regard her in a way
Not nice, not necessary to salute
In blackened tie and tears and mourning suit.

Previously Unseen

Tall Old Man

A straight man walking downstairs with his stick
Held in his right hand, holding the handrail,
Speaking slowly, his own rhetoric,
Some friendship hinted at. The tall man trailed
His feet and shortly wandered out the door
Into the street where he would make no trace.
I knew I'd seen him many times before,
Walked by yet never spoken face to face.
Was this my fault? It's true I'd not pursued
The opportunities that came my way;
Perhaps I had not pressed him, had been rude
In doing nothing more than pass the day.
Ah, well, that's in the past, for on the stair
We'd spoken and a friendly spark was there.

Delivery

I only saw his hands and judged his height
When, stopping just outside, came to the door
Sharp from his van, half-filled with lots of freight,
Confirmed I was who he was looking for.
'Sign here,' that's what he said, 'this is for you,'
And turned to climb inside, start up again,
Go on to knock on other doors, his cue
A schedule on a clipboard with a name.
I went inside, forgot about his stance,
The signing one of many more today.
If I should ever meet him, just by chance,
I wouldn't recognise him anyway.
Another human being I'd ignored!
He drives his van, deliveries on board.

Previously Unseen

Tall Girl

I drove on slowly, turning down the hill
Towards the Station, cobbles, roundabout,
Fewer people on the footpath. Still,
She is so tall and easy to pick out;
School-suited, homework in her arms,
A priestess-minded, almost-lady child.
No chewing-gum nor rancid teenage harms
Had tamed her time's tradition, nothing wild
To fight against. Her face appears subdued
By future love and pains: her rocky schemes,
High expectations, ride on fortitude,
Assure the resolution of her dreams.
All this reminds me of the day I tried
My own maturity and alloyed pride.

Different But The Same

Age, background, skin and sex and social class,

Take these away and what remains of you

And me? No more than in a silent glass

(A metaphor for living in a zoo).

So when she passed me, Asian, young and poor,

I tried to set aside concepts like these

Because dishonesty is their front door;

Behind it they control our minor pleas

For clarity, for understanding minds,

For things that lift us up from on our knees;

They push and threaten with their iron blinds.

Beside the path a row of poplar trees

Look at her as she walks uneasily,

Break out and then she'll smile at you and me.

Previously Unseen

Sunday Shopper

Nip in the air and needs for cheerful faces,
The shopping ground awash with Christmas bells,
Small children, trolleys, airs and season's graces
As well as cold December's usual smells.
Oh, get me out of here! Commerce! Its stains
Abuse us all, brings shallowness instead
Of what this season means. A man complains,
Three others nod in sympathy. One said,
"I'll get him something good this year, I will."
That's what I heard, words undermining pride;
He'd thought of someone who was rather ill
Last summer, had a stroke and almost died.
A fool I was, a stupid, stupid fool!
"Think good of all at Christmas," is the rule.

Do I know You?

You look as if I should know who you are,
For all about you, as I contemplate,
Assures me that the distance isn't far
Between us so why do I hesitate?
If I should model you in silken clay,
Carve you from wood or burnish you in brass,
Uncertainty's still present; I can't say
The image I produce is real, will last.
Your pleading tiny eyes have points of steel,
Both blackened by your parents' high distain:
Your slow, ungainly walk cannot conceal
The icy sediment within your brain.
Who are you? Still I hope you realise
You should not limit love before my eyes.

Previously Unseen

Still

The steady ladder leans against the wall.
The window cleaner hasn't far to climb.
No mountain here, no danger here at all:
The window cleaner's work is not sublime.
For twenty years or more he'd seen so much
Behind him as he'd wiped the window glass,
Cold, crystal-clear, affected by his touch
As walkers just below him pass and pass.
But no-one pays attention to his trade
To smile at him or pass the time of day;
Please, someone interrupt his neat parade,
Encourage him and recognise his way.
I wave. He looks down, stares at me;
The town clock points to twenty-five to three.

Farm Foreman

His energy, his strength, I'd always found
From morning, through the day and afternoon,
To be what made him powerful all round,
Wholesome and open, full of summer's bloom.
He spoke about his family a lot,
About his garden, how he thrived on hope,
His sporting moments, memories; forgot
His losses that were few and now remote.
But I suspected that he was unsure
Behind this all-encompassing control,
That there was something hidden, something more,
Deep down below the rooting of his soul.
Was he afraid that he would not connect
With working men who held him in respect?

Previously Unseen

Station Meeting

A football match a distance down the line
Attracted men to bond their rhyming calls
With cans of beer and wasting lots of time
Before the game and when its curtain falls.
All such behaviour justified police
Especially where women were denied
A seat upon the train and partial peace
Though she was so afraid and almost cried.
'They vandalised the coach,' she had complained,
'Rolled all about in dangerous waving flood'.
Her face agreed with this; she looked so strained
And couldn't turn away from where they stood.
I tried to listen to each anguished word
And scowled inside that men were so absurd!

Fast Mover

A turning down the side street sharply made,
He demonstrates his need to get somewhere
Where he is badly needed; sabre-blade
His left eye look, a frozen, burning stare.
Gone, leaving his remains within my sight.
A photo-shoot, a rapid, fading take,
Nobody else aware his hurried fright
Held private thoughts inside. His heart could break,
Was worried sick about the one he saw
To be no less than friendly partnership.
It was all there to see, a skin blood-raw,
Hope for him strapped on, leaving bit by drip.
Do hurry, friend, be there, outside the door,
A knock to enter, no need to do more.

Previously Unseen

Slow Man

Twice every day he locks the old house door

To go and find whatever's going on

Around about the roads and tracks he saw

The last time that he stepped unsure upon

His painful feet. His quivering dog decides

Their present route, in existential style;

Its ego and its complicated strides

Conspire to strangely change from mile to mile.

Poor man, he can't begin to understand

What's going on; his dog's the one that leads,

Confuses him, though pace does not increase;

Indeed, sometimes their onward drive might cease.

The master and his dog, fantastic team,

Drift homewards, walking through an airy dream.

Furrowed Brow

Oh, she is old, no reason to doubt;
Her face, though human, spoke out of the sun
That pounded it, the waves of wind, the drought,
The rains that came since her time had begun.
I see these aspects of her skin's terrain
A monument to living side by side
With such a military, constant strain,
A testament picked out in solemn pride.
I see her, stick and shopper, wrapped in fire,
Go slowly down her pre-determined way,
Eyes unblinking, minding no desire
Except the journey's end, no step's delay.
Your inwardness to me is not too clear
But your grained face can never disappear.

Previously Unseen

Hard-headed Builder

Well, like I said, it ain't all what it was;
The pay's not bad but when it pours and pours,
I get disheartened at such times because
We gets laid off – We're useful out-of-doors
But not at times like that, I mean to say
You just can't do it, 'cos the mortar runs
Like little babies dribbling, like, it runs
And boss gets miffed and says we've pulled a stunt
I says to him that rain is what's the reason
But he won't wear it, says we've played a trick
And never mind that rain is here this season.
The rain makes everybody sick.
So here I stand with nothing much to do
Until the bloody sun comes shining through.

Sharp Turn

Why did I pick her out from all those who
Marched up and down on Sunday afternoon?
No beauty caught my eye, no glittering shoe,
No perfect motion, gathered up in gloom.
Tight lips, cream scarf, an undetermined mind,
An empty shopping bag, plain coat and frown
All said to me that someone was unkind
To her. Who that was clearly wasn't known
By people walking past her in the street,
In all the shops, the bus, the market place,
The riverside. Her armour so complete
I was impelled to stop her, face to face
Ask who it was, who did this; but instead
I turned away, buried my heart and fled.

Previously Unseen

Second Time Around

She had a staged career so sensitive,
Her art a challenge to her mind's release,
So much in talent there, so very much to give
That rest was not a thing to bring her ease.
Then, understanding that the days had burned,
She ditched the drama, took to slighter things,
A family, lost to the craze, returned,
And self-indulgence fit for kings.
Well, as this novel phase took over her
And happiness more real painted her face
A sudden panic spiked this new future;
An illness scratched this simple grace.
We need an end that's comforting, be
In first-class seating through eternity.

Helmet

Sometimes the less you see the more you see,
As images and colours intervene
So when he waved his helmet-head at me
I knew the motorcyclist, not the dream.
Not knowing is a steady-state domain
For most of us with secular concern
But his assent, unqualified and plain
Ensured my passage, tempered my concern.
From east to west he steered the large, black bike
Through traffic fumes along the contra-flow,
Not pleasant in the least, its waving spike
A scary place for anyone to go.
And yet, when waiting in the line,
He nodded, so he is a friend of mine.

Previously Unseen

Assisting

The lady with the lapel badge is staff,
Cares for the residents who come from all
Around the area. She makes them laugh;
Though few can stand, she makes them feel so tall.
I am amazed that she can be like this
Day after day and not betray true charm
While working with the elderly. To miss
A chance to lift their spirits, make hearts warm
Is not her way. Yet I can't understand
What drives her on to wipe out misery,
What power she has to wave her magic wand,
Dismiss soiled beds and smells and stale tea.
The whole room wanted her to carry on;
Laughs followed her but stopped when she had gone.

Man on a Cambridge Bus

Contemporary clothing, snug and mild,
Tightly fits his bulky body. Bling,
A mighty prop to camouflage this child
Confines his body – Thinks he is a king.
Smoothes his phone with gentle finger ends,
Ignores the passengers and needs to hide,
Keeps polishing his phone and sometimes bends
His face towards the window at the side.
But I can see his heart is so afraid
And immature and insecure and thin.
This person should be living on parade
But hides behind an armour-plated skin.
The bus stops so he stands to march away
Invisibly: There's nothing more to say.

Previously Unseen

Meetings

On the way to school this morning's sky
Had silenced all the street like heavy mist.
A chance look through the window; stopping by
A car unloaded youngsters who resist
The coming day's attention but just then
The smallest of them suddenly leapt high,
Was bouncing in a dance, again, again,
On seeing that his friend was coming by.
Just like the new connections every day
In airport flight arrivals; long-lost friends
In overwhelming joy can hug and sway,
To tie together once more, make amends.
For parting's no sweet sorrow, always pain,
Whilst meeting switches life to go again.

Meter Reader

He grinds from door to door, from street to street,
Employed to do this, get the numbers down;
Not keen to talk much with the folk he'll meet,
Polite in function, never seen to frown.
Mostly a drifter, sees what's going on
In homes in back streets, new estates; all hold
A scattering of meters passed and gone,
Soon scored and read and stored. Untold
Numbers of customers concede to him,
Allow him entry, search beneath the stair.
They know precisely where they should begin
To demonstrate the spot that calls him there.
He sniffs, shines straight his torch, nods, turns away.
It's just a job – There's nothing more to say.

Previously Unseen

No-Car Man

Three bikes, all different but really the same,
Each of them useful to this worn-down man
To get him into town and back again,
Not quickly, though, but since the days began
To make his heart beat faster for his wife
Whose kindly help had closer made their ties,
Develop strange new meanings in his life
And make the pulse of loving slowly rise.
How wonderful to watch an ordinary man
And woman come to meet at this rock face,
Turn to each other as they both began
To understand that at this little place
The past and present light the hours to come.
The bicycles unite them, one to one.

Not a Real Face

Bright blue sky, sunlight in the wintertime
Carrying clear joy as out to sea,
The coloured earth contrasting as the shine
Rebounds upon the road and over me.
The lonely path to town beside the road,
The ditch and lines of stubble everywhere,
Were empty till somebody slowly strode
My way, a teenage girl with wavy hair.
I cycled by and looked into her eyes:
They coldly indicated, 'Look away!'
This tough instruction came as no surprise
For youth is often insecure today.
Layers of make-up armoured her around
As did her i-phone's taut metallic sound.

Previously Unseen

A Shy Smile

She sat down at the far side of the room,
Hardly noticed as she settled there,
Admitting to no stuffy, curtained gloom,
A fine old lady, lightness in her hair.
A few words such as these give slight content,
Describing nothing deep within her heart
So I must now explain just what I meant,
Express the insights, each and every part.
All I can say about the little seen
Of her real character, her sense of life,
Is limited by what there might have been
Had I but known her when words were rife
But now she sits alone and hours complete
Melt gently as her smile defies defeat.

Written Round Her Head

It wasn't how she looked, her style, her clothes,
That signalled her intentions for the day
Nor was it who was with her; heaven knows,
It was written on her headband. It did say,
'God is…' and I could not make out the rest,
The right conclusion that the statement told.
The colour, well, I missed it, failed that test
Although the text seemed letters flaming gold.
Still she was there when I walked back that way
With friends, a couple, happily engaged
In conversation fitting for that time of day.
The scene ongoing – Time to leave the stage.
What did it say? I almost stopped to ask,
Decided not to – Kept up to my task.

Previously Unseen

Amman Father

A small explosion rising from the ground,
A land-mine bomb. The small child staggered, snapped
And crumpled. Father ran and caught her, found
A hospital. Surgeons swiftly mapped
Her situation, operated on
Her supine body till a long, deep rest
Assured her life, though injuries had gone
Into her heart. Nobody could have guessed
How parts of her would come to understand
The wide degree of unremitting calm
She needed. Nobody would see her stand
To maybe face once more the hidden harm
And yet her father's smile spread
Her spirit north and south within her head.

Winter-flowering Jasmine

One person only walked the narrow mall,
A shopping bag wrapped round his drooping hand.
He stopped and turned and stared straight at a wall,
Quite mesmerised by winter jasmine fanned
Widely and flowering a yellowy cascade.
What was there, clutching at his eye, his mind?
This out-of-season shrub stood on parade
Like him so long ago? Did he there find
Small echoes of a military man?
Perhaps, but that is guesswork, insecure.
Now he walks on to town, his measured plan,
The winter-flowering jasmine and its lure
Brushed off as, bag close-gripped, with even pace
He catches up, tomorrow on his face.

Previously Unseen

On Palace Green

On Palace Green, one lazy Saturday,

When golden leaves mottled the rain-free walk

And shoppers passed and looked along the way,

She stood a moment, paused as if to talk,

While autumn sun in levelled rays sought out

Her even face that, wrapped in gentle wool,

Now hardly moved: her eyes slid round about

While in her mind she loved the moment's lull.

But just as I began to join her song

She walked on past, some shopping in her mind;

The market place attractions would belong

To what she thought. I guessed that she would find

Enough to carry home and to forget

That single moment when we almost met.

Parking Meter Man

We'd never met before, might not again,
The meter man and I, both armed to fight
The raw night air, the cold, the wind, the rain
Attacking both of us that autumn night.
I knew my time was up when he stood close
To where my car was parked. Inside he peered
To check his hand-held overdue device
Confirming all about him that I feared.
'Please, my new ticket, here it is,' I said
In futile hope that he would change his mind.
He looked not in my anxious face; instead
He cancelled the excess – Was he blind?
'That's all right, sir,' He said, and moved along,
Proved all my expectations had been wrong.

Previously Unseen

Piercing Look

He faced me head on straight and blinked not once,

Grey curls, an always-outdoors head; his skin

Graced by a maggot's patch of missed-off chance,

A time-tuned fool whose yesterdays might win.

But that was long ago; the look again

Convinces me, had formed some strong intent

To take a chance, accept the slurry drain

He fell into was not what he had meant.

Things do go wrong, of that we both agree,

For no-one sits upon a cloud for long,

And some fight back while others drown at sea,

No matter that they shout, want to belong.

He's staring still, though I am out of sight,

Can in his hand and gagging for a fight.

Predatory Owl

The bird looked at the people's masquerade,
To left, to right and up and down and then
I waited for her to select her prey,
Someone she knew, somebody over there,
A friend she hoped to meet sometime today.
The owl ignored them all, flew through the air
On fragile feet, for age had given way
To carefulness. Perhaps it was her look,
Her stealthy minute movements down the street,
Made me to step behind her, watch her flight,
Her mind my occupation till her feet
Stopped once again, turn sharply to the right,
Go down the passage leading to her lair,
Her nesting place, her tea, her comfy chair.

Previously Unseen

Quizzical Look

Our eyebrows are perceptive, all their lines
Move clearly, indicate what's going on.
That lady's were in tune, their soft inclines
Milled perfectly - Had they not been so strong
I never would have notice her. Her still
And constant pinned-down look tightly controlled
Yet searching me till she had had her fill,
No matter that I, too, was forward, bold
And seeking in her gaze some chance to link
Myself to her, a chance to answer back.
A winning pass, she might begin to sink
And turn away? My fumbling, walking track
Reached home. The key turns slowly; once again
I see those eyebrows slide before her brain.

Runner

With narrow hips and shoulders rather broad,
A military background; he was fast
And corporately running in accord
With Ely Runners' logo on his mast.
Along the Fenland river banks and droves
We pattered in our training harmony,
Discussing, between breaths, new running shoes
That might assist our distance parody.
However, he had no special desire
To finish in the leading echelon,
But looked around to see the world on fire .
While other runners dreamed their marathon.
His concentration plan leaked right away.
He's not fast but he did enjoy the day.

Previously Unseen

Ice Queen

The annual fair set in the public place,
Mid-February, high clouds moving by,
Lit up the town, the streaming human pace
Encouraged by excitement built a cry.
The tent sucked in a queue of arid charm,
All ages shuffled cold feet into thrills
Much colder than the coldest night-time warm
Can offer, negatively, late-night chills.
The wavering way took bodies closely past
A swim-suit lady, trim and well-endowed,
Encased in blocks of ice, stuck still, stuck fast,
Ice barrier between her and the crowd.
Warm breath from each appeared and nicely blurred
Our dreamy prisons where our senses stirred.

Contents

Anybody There? 7

Was He Spanish? 8

At the Railway Station 9

Up and Down the Street 10

Trolley Collector 11

Builder's Mate 12

Chip Van Man 13

The Italian 14

Such Long and Curly Hair 15

Street Musician 16

Dog walking man 17

Fen Dweller 18

Small Car Lady Driver 19

Skip With A Rope 20

Garden Bicycle 21

Going Home From School 22

Sitting in the window 23

Housebound 24

Scrap Metal Collector 25

Shop Keeper 26

Ice Cream Seller 27

Lady with a following Dog 28

Man in a Boat 29

Man with Bad Leg 30

Mobility Scooter Lady 31

Young Lady on a Bus 32

A Priest without Pride 33

Agency Nurse 34

Wrinkles 35

Olives 36

Horticultural Assistant 37

On Mummy's Knee 38

Home Worker 39

Ornithologist 40

Pony and Trap Man 41

Reader 42

Ancient Cyclist 43

Wellington Boots 44

Waiting 45

Assistant 46

Tyre Fitter 47

Bad Feet 48

Two on a Wall, Sitting 49

Blotched Look 50

Brightly Clad Lady 51

Two Miles Away 52

Three Dogs 53

By the Shop Window 54

Child in a car 55

The Observer 56

Taxi Driver 57

Dark Glasses 58

Dead Ducks 59

Spirit buyer 60

Fear 61

Slim, Long Hair 62

Furrowed Forehead 63

Shop Front 64

Hair In Waves 65

Lady Musing 66

Long-Coated Lady 67

Melodeon Man 68

Newspaper Man 69

Young Man in a Public House 70

A mobile phone 71

On Every Road	72
Aglow	73
Old Lady, Shopping Trolley	74
House to Let	75
Only A Farmer	76
Poser	77
Saxophonist	78
In the Charity Shop	79
In The Doctor's Waiting Room	80
Jogger	81
Background	82
Unnoticed	83
Two Polystyrene Coffee Cups	84
Be Gone	85
Thin Young Man	86
Restaurant Assistant	87
Tennis Player	88
Crime Stopper	89
Dispensing	90
Swagger	91
Slight and Dark	92
Garage Owner	93

Hat Lady 94

Selling Shoes 95

Man Outside The Shop 96

Mill Man 97

Zebra Crossing Incident 98

A Kind of Politician 99

Adonis in Trainers 100

Writer 101

An Unexpected Meeting 102

When Not Working 103

Passing Through 104

Pouring Rain Lady 105

Premature Baby 106

In the Distance – A Horse 107

Antiques Young Man 108

Well Done 109

At the Bank 110

W. I. Husband 111

Two Sticks 112

Baseball Cap 113

Tight-lipped 114

By the Shop Door 115

Theatrical Man 116

Caretaker 117

The Same Way 118

Checkout Angel 119

Cinema 120

The End of School 121

The Drinker 122

The Big Screen 123

Crew-cut Lady 124

Tall On high Heels 125

Dead Shop Lady 126

Tall Old Man 127

Delivery 128

Tall Girl 129

Different But The Same 130

Sunday Shopper 131

Do I know You? 132

Still 133

Farm Foreman 134

Station Meeting 135

Fast Mover 136

Slow Man 137

Furrowed Brow 138

Hard-headed Builder 139

Sharp Turn 140

Second Time Around 141

Helmet 142

Assisting 143

Man on a Cambridge Bus 144

Meetings 145

Meter Reader 146

No-Car Man 147

Not a Real Face 148

A Shy Smile 149

Written Round Her Head 150

Amman Father 151

Winter-flowering Jasmine 152

On Palace Green 153

Parking Meter Man 154

Piercing Look 155

Predatory Owl 156

Quizzical Look 157

Runner 158

Ice Queen 159